opposites

**Photography
George Siede and Donna Preis**

Louis Weber, C.E.O.
Publications International, Ltd.
7373 North Cicero Avenue
Lincolnwood, Illinois 60646

ISBN 0–7853–1280–3

Publications International, Ltd.

off

on

on

off

on

off

in
out

in   out

in

out

front
back

back

front

back   front

open
closed

open closed

closed

open

up
down

up

down

down

up

stop
go

stop

go

stop

go

big
small

big

small

small

big

over
under

over

under

over

under

left
right

left   right

left

right